Celebrating your year

1961

a very special year for

_____

_____

_____

_____

_____

A message from the author:

Welcome to the year 1961.

I trust you will enjoy this fascinating romp down memory lane.

And when you have reached the end of the book, please join me in the battle against AI generated copy-cat books and fake reviews.

Details are near the back of the book.

Best regards,
Bernard Bradforsand-Tyler.

Contents

1961 Family Life in the USA 8
Life in the United Kingdom 14
Our Love Affair with Cars 19
Tuning in to Television 24
Most Popular TV Shows of 1961 25
Dick Van Dyke & Mary Tyler Moore 28
JFK 35th President of the USA 30
The Cold War–Nuclear Arms Race 33
The Cold War–Space Race 34
Space Race Inspired Movies 36
Cuba Invasion at Bay of Pigs 37
    Berlin Builds a Wall 38
    The Cold War–Battlefield Vietnam 39
    Freedom Riders Against Segregation . . . 41
    World Wildlife Fund Created 43
    1961 in Cinema and Film 45
Top Grossing Films of the Year . . 47
West Side Story Hits Cinemas . . . 48
The Gossip Magazines 49
Who Were the Rat Pack? 52
    Musical Memories 53
    1961 Billboard Top 30 Songs 54
    Fashion Trends of the 1960s 57
    Also in Sports 66
Science and Medicine 67
Other News from 1961 68
Famous People Born in 1961 72
1961 in Numbers 76
Image Attributions 84

Advertisement

No fuss. No figuring. No delay.
Just aim and shoot in sun or shade... Automatic Electric Eye does the rest...
Never before a Fully Automatic Electric Eye Camera with built-in flash at this sensationally low price. New Tower Automatic 127 $17.50.

At last, a low-cost camera designed to give you every automatic feature found on more expensive cameras of its type. PLUS brand new features not found on *any* camera in its price range.

Take 12 color or black and white pictures or color slides on inexpensive 127 film. Take them outdoors or indoors... day or night-time. No extra flash gun to buy or carry. Built-in flash uses new jellybean-size AGI bulbs.

Remarkable photoelectric eye sets lens automatically for correct daytime exposures. When you focus for flash shots, the lens adjusts to the correct opening automatically... No time wasted dividing distance and guide numbers.

It even tells you *when* to use the flash. When light is too dim for regular shots, you see a red warning signal in the viewfinder. Neck strap included.

Let's flashback to 1961, a very special year.

Was this the year you were born?

Was this the year you were married?

Whatever the reason, this book is a celebration of your year,

THE YEAR 1961.

Turn the pages to discover a book packed with fun-filled fabulous facts. We look at the people, the places, the politics and the pleasures that made 1961 unique and helped shape the world we know today.

So get your time-travel suit on, and enjoy this trip down memory lane, to rediscover what life was like, back in the year 1961.

1961 Family Life in the USA

Imagine if time-travel was a reality, and one fine morning you wake up to find yourself flashed back in time, back to the year 1961.

What would life be like for a typical family, in a typical town, somewhere in America?

Artist's impression of a family enjoying leisure activities in the early '60s.

We often reminisce about the golden boom years of the '50s and '60s, when families flourished, babies were born in record numbers, unemployment was low, and our standard of living surpassed that which our parents could only dream of.

By the year 1961, the economy was stronger than it had ever been, and as a nation we had 30% more purchasing power than ten years earlier. Although we made up just 6% of the world's population, we consumed a whopping one-third of the world's goods and services.[1] A culture of consume and discard flourished, driven by an advertising industry which instilled in us the belief that we constantly needed more and more, bigger and better.

[1] exploros.com/summary/Economy-in-the-1950s.

The start of the decade marked a high point for the Baby Boomer generation (1946-1964). Children under nineteen represented 38% of our nation,[1] a percentage which has been in decline ever since.

Family life was everything, as the first of the Baby Boomers became teenagers. The single income family was still the norm, with fathers commuting to work while mothers were encouraged to stay at home.

Artist's impression of a typical suburban family in the early 1960s.

One-third of us now lived in the suburbs, having fled the decaying cities for the dream of a house on our own land, a car, a dog and 2.3 kids. 80% of households owned an automobile. The 40-hour workweek with paid leave had become the norm and we spent more on leisure activities, health care and education than ever before.

[1] census.gov/library/publications/1963/compendia/statab/84ed.html, page 6.

Advertisement

Modernize your kitchen with *Flair* by Frigidaire!
Looks built-in...but you can install it within minutes!

Modernize your kitchen with Flair by Frigidaire!
Looks built-in...but you can install it within minutes!

Costs no more than an ordinary range—as little as $4.15 a week! Sensational new Flair by Frigidaire brings built-in beauty to your home—in a free-standing Range. Flair gives you surface and oven cooking in one compact unit.

Just slides into place of your old electric range after it's attached to the optional cabinet or your own custom-built cabinet. Choice of 4 models in 2 sizes: 40-inch, double oven; 30-inch, single oven.

All the features of highest-priced conventional range. Eye-level ovens; Hand-High Surface Units; Heat-Minder makes every utensil automatic; Speed-Heat Surface Unit shortens cooking time.

Roll-to-You Cooking Top—slides out of sight. Most convenient space-saving electric range ever! Surface units are easy to clean. Lift up and stay up! Porcelain enamel Drip Bowls.

Advertisement

She's smart! She's thrifty! She saves... America's most valuable stamps.

Join the 27,000,000 smart, thrifty women who earn the best values with S & H Green Stamps.

Good housekeeping guarantees performance of America's only nationwide stamp plan.

For women, marriage and children were still the priority. Most women aged 30-34 were married (88%) and the majority (90%) had children.[1]

Working women could expect to be paid almost 40% less than their male counterparts. It was universally accepted that a man was the breadwinner of the family, and that a wife should earn less.

Mother with daughters cooking, 1961.

The median family income was $5,700 a year.[2] Unemployment stood at 6%, with GDP growth at 2.3%.[3]

Average costs in 1961 [4]	
New house	$19,365
New car	$2,850
Refrigerator	$300
Vacuum cleaner	$45
A gallon of gasoline	$0.31

[1] From the US Census Bureau-1960 Census: Population, Supplementary Reports: Marital Status of the Population.
[2] census.gov/library/publications/1962/demo/p60-038.html.
[3] thebalance.com/unemployment-rate-by-year-3305506.
[4] thepeoplehistory.com and mclib.info/reference/local-history-genealogy/historic-prices/.

But beyond the glamour and excesses of our pristine, appliance-filled suburban lives, there was another America. One where struggles with poverty, health care, education, housing, racial and sexual inequality, and even the right to vote were brewing the demand for change. We took to the streets in record numbers—demanding to be heard, demanding change for a better, more egalitarian America. The 1960s would become the decade of reform and revolution.

American civil rights protests in the early '60s.

And adding to the unrest, the threat of Cold War was an ever-present concern. The Cold War dominated US policies and communist fears gripped the nation throughout the decade and beyond.

By the start of 1961, the USA and USSR were stockpiling nuclear weapons at a frenzied pace. And space exploration was turning outer-space into the next Cold War battleground. The Nuclear Arms Race and the Space Race were in full swing.

We would endure another 35 years of tension between the two super-powers before the Cold War finally ended with the dissolution of the Soviet Union in 1991.

Life in the United Kingdom

Now just imagine you flashed back to a town in 1961 England or Western Europe.

Unlike their lavish, consumer-driven counterparts in America, a very different picture would await you.

By 1961, the United Kingdom was still struggling to regain its place on the world stage. It was no longer a superpower having lost that title, along with many of its former colonies, in the aftermath of the second world war. Rebuilding from the ruins of war had exacted a heavy economic toll on the country.

London "Bobby" helping kids cross the street.

It would be a few more years before the cultural revolution of the Swinging Sixties would, through music, fashion and the arts, place Britain once again at the center of the world.

In the years leading up to 1961, the UK, like much of the western world, enjoyed low unemployment (around 2%), real wage increases, and growth in consumer spending. There was spare money for spending on some luxuries and leisure pursuits. Prime Minister Harold MacMillan famously summed it up when he stated, "you've never had it so good".[1]

Piccadilly Circus in the early '60s.

Yet this apparent prosperity masked the relative decline of British competitiveness on the world stage. The UK had slipped behind its European neighbors and did not come close to the lavish consumerism of the USA.

[1] nationalarchives.gov.uk/education/resources/fifties-britain/youve-never-good/.

Advertisement

Stop, look and list 'em! 12 extra features never before assembled in any portable under $100! New Monarch portable by Remington costs less than $90.

Monarch's 12 Extra Features: 1. Single key instantly sets or clears columns and indents! 2. Two-Color ribbon and stencil control! 3. Erasure table on cylinder simplifies making corrections! 4. Removable top cover makes ribbon cleaning easier! 5. Calibrated scale on paper ball lets you center your headings faster! 6. Numerals and calibrations on paper table simplify margin settings positively! 7. Card and writing line scale lets you type more precisely! 8. Adjustable paper edge guide lets you insert paper precisely every time! 9. Variable line spacer lets you type "right on the lines" of ruled paper! 10. Carriage centering device locks machine tight for safer carrying. 11. Touch regulator adjusts to your individual "feel"! 12. Lighter weight without a hint of flimsiness or "creep" while you type!

Monarch is the newest model in the complete quality line of portables by Remington. You get precision–easy action and crisper, cleaner print-work even if you never typed before. And all Remington portables come complete with carrying case, typing course and chart, free of extra cost. 4 out of 5 typewriter advances come from Remington.

By 1961, private car ownership was still rare, and most households continued to rely on public transport. In fact, steam trains continued to run until the mid-'60s. Similarly, road networks and telecommunications remained woefully inadequate.

Post war Britain had borrowed heavily from USA and Canada in order to survive and rebuild. Yet Britain failed to modernize its industries in the same way France, Germany, and other war-torn countries had succeeded in doing.

Early '60s photo of lady on a double-decker bus.

From within this bleak and conservative nation a new generation was soon to explode. Within a few short years, they would shake the world. British youth would lead the cultural revolution of the '60s and London would be their epicenter.

The Beatles with Ed Sullivan. From left Ringo Starr, George Harrison, Ed Sullivan, John Lennon, and Paul McCartney, 9th February 1964.

Advertisement

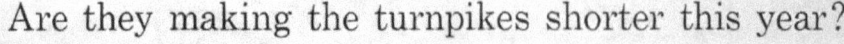

61 PLYMOUTH...SOLID BEAUTY

Are they making the turnpikes shorter this year?

Take that next trip in a '61 Plymouth. This Solid Beauty will give you a feeling that roads have never been so smooth, horizons so easy to catch. Everything about this low-price car takes you there in new comfort. It's easy to get in, easy to sit in, easy to see out of. Its quiet one-piece welded Unibody is snug and tight. Its Torsion-Aire suspension (no extra cost) takes practically all the sway and dip out of driving. Plymouth is smoothing the kinks out of the miles. Let your Plymouth dealer show you how.

61 Plymouth... Solid Beauty

Our Love Affair with Cars

By 1961, 63.2 million cars were on our roads. And with more and more cars purchased each year, owning a car was no longer considered a luxury reserved only for the wealthy.

Artists image of young adults around a 1961 Pontiac Grand Prix.

Increased car ownership and the creation of the National Highway System gave us a new sense of freedom. Office commuters could live further out from city centers and commute quickly and comfortably to work. The suburbanization of America, which began in the early '50s, now saw one-third of Americans living in the suburbs. Furthermore, rural areas were no longer isolated, benefiting from access to food, medical and other supplies.

Services related businesses such as drive-through or drive-in restaurants and drive-in cinemas were commonplace and popular, especially among the younger generation.

[1] fhwa.dot.gov/ohim/summary95/mv200.pdf.

An astonishing one in six working adults were employed directly or indirectly by the American automobile industry.

1961 Chrysler Newport.

Detroit was America's car manufacturing powerhouse, where "the Big Three" (Ford, General Motors and Chrysler) produced year-on-year bigger, longer, and heavier gas-guzzlers to satisfy the midcentury consumer desire for style over efficiency and safety. Decorative chrome and tail fins reached new heights towards the end of the '50s. However, by the early '60s, the consumer mentality was turning against this extravagance and excess.

Led in part by the success of the imported Volkswagen Beetle and the economic recession of 1958, consumer demand began shifting towards smaller, more compact, cheaper and safer vehicles. The scene was set for Japanese small car manufacturers to take on the Big Three.

Four car-producing countries dominated in 1961: England, France, and Germany, with America in the top spot. However, this elite group would soon be rocked by the aggressive expansion of the Japanese automotive industry. Within 5 years, Japan would rise to become the third largest car producing country, behind only Germany and the US.

Last one to conk out is a Volkswagen.

1961 European car advertisements for Renault Dauphine, Morris Minor 1000, and Volkswagen.

Car ownership in other countries lagged behind the USA, even with the rising incomes and living standards of most western nations. Public transport was still the norm for European and British commuters.

In Asia, the car had yet to become mainstream. Less than 1% of the population in China and India could afford a car.

Before you buy any low-priced car... drive the new F-85.
It's every inch an Oldsmobile!

Take the wheel of this smaller-size Oldsmobile... and you'll feel the difference a full eight cylinders make! Here's zesty, man-size action, from the exclusive Rockette V-8–the 155-horsepower aluminum engine, standard at no extra cost! Here's gas economy you'd expect from smaller cars... nimbleness in traffic... handy length for easy parking. But inside, you get ample room for six with big-car solidness for relaxing comfort! Size up the delightful-to-drive new F-85... the hot new number in the low-price field!

Oldsmobile division * General Motors Corporation.
Built for the buyer who wants something better in a smaller car!

Advertisement

A NEW NETWORK OF SERVICE STATIONS, GOING AMERICA-WIDE,

BRINGS YOU A FREE LOCAL INFORMATION SERVICE AS YOU TRAVEL

THE NATION'S HIGHWAYS THIS SUMMER—"AS YOU TRAVEL—ASK US!"

When you get behind the wheel, keep an eye peeled for the friendly signs that say "As you travel—ask us," under the red, white and blue Torch and Oval. There you'll find a specially-trained service station dealer who will point out places to eat, places to stay, places to see and places to play. This kind of local information will make you feel that you're among friends. And you will be.

©1961 AMERICAN OIL COMPANY

Travel the American Way
A new network of service stations, going America-wide
brings you a free local information service as you travel
the nation's highways this summer—"as you travel—ask us!"

When you get behind the wheel, keep an eye peeled for the friendly signs that say "As you travel—ask us," under the red, white and blue Torch and Oval. There you'll find a specially-trained service station dealer who will point out places to eat, places to stay, places to see and places to play. This kind of local information will make you feel that you're among friends. And you will be.

Tuning in to Television

Television ownership in America soared during the '50s and early '60s, increasing sharply from only 9% of households in 1950, to 89% by 1961. During the '50s, television's "Golden Age", most of the programs were broadcast live from New York in the ongoing tradition of old-time radio broadcasting. But by the '60s, made-for-TV programs coming out of Los Angeles dominated our screens.

By 1961, the three national US television networks were able to reach the most remote parts of the country, bringing a shared common experience to both urban and rural America. Television had quickly become our preferred source of entertainment and information.

TV time in 1961.

Elsewhere in the world, access to television was not nearly as widespread as in the US. Due to the extreme costs of setting up networks and financing programs, many countries did not begin television broadcasts until the mid-'60s or later.

In many countries, television networks were government owned or subsidized. This allowed for more focus on serious documentaries and news broadcasts, without the constant concern of generating advertising revenue.

Most Popular TV Shows of 1961

1	Wagon Train	11	My Three Sons
2	Bonanza	12	The Garry Moore Show
3	Gunsmoke	13	Rawhide
4	Hazel	14	The Real McCoys
5	Perry Mason	15	Lassie
6	The Red Skelton Show	=	Sing Along with Mitch
7	The Andy Griffith Show	17	Dennis the Menace
8	The Danny Thomas Show	18	Ben Casey
9	Dr. Kildare	19	The Ed Sullivan Show
10	Candid Camera	20	Car 54, Where Are You?

* From Nielsen Media Research 1961-'62 season of top-rated primetime television series in the USA.

Quiz shows, sitcoms, and variety programs remained ever popular in 1961, while drama, kids' shows, news and sports programs added to the mix. But the Wild West continued to pull the highest ratings, with the top three programs of 1961 being Westerns.

James Arness & Susan Cummings in *Gunsmoke,* 1960 (CBS. 1955-1975).

Based on the long running radio show of the same name, *Gunsmoke* aired for 20 seasons from 1955-'75. It held the top spot of Most Popular TV Show for four straight years from 1957 to 1960.

Robert Horton and Ward Bond in *Wagon Train,* 1962 (NBC. 1957-'62, ABC. 1962-'65).

Clint Eastwood received his first big acting break when he was cast as Rowdy Yates in the TV Western *Rawhide* (CBS. 1959-1965). The series would run for eight seasons, reaching peak ratings in 1960-1961.

Richard Chamberland in *Dr. Kildaire* (NBC. 1961-1966).

Connie Hines and Alan Young in *Mister Ed* (CBS. 1961-1966).

The television networks were quick to turn out new programs to keep us tuning in. Here are just a few of the new programs that aired for the first time in 1961: *Dr. Kildaire, Mister Ed, Ben Casey, Password, ABC's Wide World of Sports, The Dick Van Dyke Show,* and *Four Corners* (Australia) which is still on the air today.

Vince Edwards with guest star Tuesday Weld in *Ben Casey* (ABC. 1961-1966).

Allen Ludden host of game show *Password* (CBS. 1961-'67, ABC 1971-'75).

Advertisement

New Sylvania TV reflects nothing but quality!

...in new Reflection-Free Picture—Gone are the glassy reflections that clutter the screen on ordinary TV. On new Sylvania TV you see the whole picture and nothing but the picture, thanks to the "satin finish" of Sylvania shatterproof safety screen.

...in new Woodblend HaloLight—This exclusive "picture frame" of cool white light makes viewing so much easier and more enjoyable. When the set is off, HaloLight turns off and changes to a warm beige woodtone that blends with the cabinet.

...in Handsome Hardwood Cabinets—Shown here is the new "Fascination" console by Heywood-Wakefield. It typifies the grace and good taste you'll find in all Sylvania TV. See Sylvania Reflection-Free TV in 23" and 19" models at your dealer's.

"Fascination Model 23C38. Solid birch cabinet by Heywood-Wakefield. Hand-rubbed walnut finish. Beautiful tambour doors."

Dick Van Dyke & Mary Tyler Moore   3rd October 1961

Mary Tyler Moore, Dick Van Dyke & Larry Mathews in *The Dick Van Dyke Show* (CBS. 1961-1966).

Two of our most celebrated screen legends launched their TV careers when *The Dick Van Dyke Show* aired in 1961.

The CBS sitcom ran for five seasons, following the lives of suburban couple Rob and Laura Petrie (Dick Van Dyke and Mary Tyler Moore).

The 158 half-hour episodes centered around family life in the suburbs with their son Richie, and Rob's work as a comedy writer for the fictitious *Alan Brady Show*.

The series was filmed before a live TV audience, one of the few to do so at the time. It picked up a total of fifteen Emmy awards during its five years, with Van Dyke winning three awards for Lead Actor in a Series, and Moore winning two awards for Lead Actress in a Series.

Van Dyke had previously worked on radio and Broadway before moving to TV. He went on to star in numerous Hollywood musicals, comedies and dramatic films, notably *Bye Bye Birdie* (1963), *Mary Poppins* (1964), *Chitty Chitty Bang Bang* (1968), *The Comic* (1969), and *A Night at the Museum* (2006).

Moore had guest-starred on numerous television programs before landing the role of Laura Petrie at the age of 24.

The enduring quality of *The Dick Van Dyke Show* led to numerous spin-off television series in later years.

The New Dick Van Dyke Show (CBS. 1971-1974) saw Van Dyke joined by an entirely different cast.

Dick Van Dyke, Hope Lange, Angela Powell & Michael Shea in *The New Dick Van Dyke Show* (CBS. 1971-1974).

Valerie Harper, Ed Asner, Cloris Leachman, Gavin MacLeod, Mary Tyler Moore and Ted Knight studio publicity photo for *The Mary Tyler Moore Show*.

Tyler Moore's popularity secured her a stand-alone sitcom *The Mary Tyler Moore Show* (CBS. 1970-1977). The popular TV series won a total of 29 Emmys during its seven-year run, a record unbeaten until 2002 by NBC's sitcom *Frasier*.

Spin-offs from *The Mary Tyler Moore Show* include *Rhoda* (CBS. 1974-78), *Phyllis* (CBS. 1975-77) and *Lou Grant* (CBS. 1977-82).

Van Dyke has been honored with numerous Tony and Emmy Awards in his lifetime, as well as a Career Achievement award (Television Critics Association, 2003) and a Lifetime Achievement award (Screen Actors Guild, 2013). In 1995 he was inducted into the Television Hall of Fame.

Moore has received a total of seven Emmy Awards over the years. In 1986 she was inducted into the Television Hall of Fame. She also received a Lifetime Achievement Award in Comedy (American Comedy Awards, 1987).

JFK 35th President of the USA

20th January 1961

"Ask not what your country can do for you, ask what you can do for your country."

John F. Kennedy's inspirational and memorable words resonate as strongly with Americans today as they did when he spoke them at the closing of his inaugural address. On 20th January 1961, Kennedy was sworn in as the 35th President of the USA, becoming America's first Roman Catholic President, and youngest elected President at the time.

John F. Kennedy giving his inaugural address from the balcony of the Capitol Building.

Nearly one million people braved subfreezing temperatures to catch a glimpse of our charismatic new President. His inaugural address focused on America's role on the international stage at a time when Cold War fears dominated our lives. In acknowledging the dangers of the communist threat and the Nuclear Arms Race, Kennedy gave us hope and confidence in America's ability to balance power with peace.

The speech and the parade to the White House was the first to be telecast live in color, reaching a viewing audience of millions.

Frank Sinatra welcomes the President and First Lady to the Inaugural Ball at the National Guard Armory in Washington DC. 19th Jan 1961.

Frank Sinatra and actor Peter Lawford hosted a pre-inaugural ball on the eve of Inauguration. Billed as one of the biggest parties ever held in the state, Broadway suspended shows for the evening so invited guests could be present. Many stars of the stage and screen attended, with performances by Sidney Poitier, Nat King Cole, Ella Fitzgerald, Gene Kelly, Jimmy Durante, Harry Belafonte, Milton Berle, and others.

During his first year in office, Kennedy established the Peace Corps, a state funded organization which trained young American volunteers for deployment in foreign nations on two or three-year terms, with the goal of assisting in community development.

Asked "what you can do for your country," thousands volunteered. By the end of 1961, the first 750 recruits were sent to 13 developing nations, to promote peace, friendship, development, and American-style democracy. By the end of 1963, 7000 volunteers were serving in 44 third-world countries.

To date, the Peace Corps has aided more that 140 nations worldwide.

Kennedy's assassination on 22nd November 1963 cut short the life of one of America's most loved Presidents. His two years in office focused mainly on America's tense relations with Cuba and the Soviets, work which his successor, Lyndon B. Johnson, continued.

President Kennedy's popularity was in part due to the celebrity status given to him and his beautiful wife Jacqueline, by magazines and television, such as was normally reserved for movie or pop stars.

Advertisement

Good coffee is like friendship: rich and warm and strong.

Coffee is the life of the party.
Nothing else comes close.
So make it extra-good every time: dark-rich and rewarding.
With a heaping tablespoon of coffee for every friendly cup.

Make it coffee. Make it often. Make it right.

The Cold War–Nuclear Arms Race

Cold War tensions between the two former allies–the USSR and the USA–had been building during the 1950s and dominated our lives throughout the 1960s.

Starting in the USA as policies for communist containment, the distrust and misunderstanding between the two sides quickly escalated from political squabbling, into a military nuclear arms race. Trillions of dollars in military spending saw both sides stockpile their nuclear arsenals, strategically positioning and pointing their missiles closer and closer to the other.

By 1961, the USA had a stockpile of 22,229 nuclear weapons, against the Soviet's 2,471 weapons.[1] The UK was the only other nation in this elite group, with 70 weapons.

30th October– The Soviets tested a massive hydrogen bomb known as Big Ivan (Tsar Bomba) over the Novaya Zemlya island in the Arctic. The test served to prove the Soviet's nuclear superiority, to counter the larger stockpile of weapons held by the USA.

Big Ivan was 1,400 times more powerful than the WWII bombs dropped on Hiroshima and Nagasaki. It weighed 27 metric tons, with a nuclear yield of 55-60 megatons of TNT. By comparison, the largest US nuclear device ever tested yielded 15 megatons.

Big Ivan remains the most powerful human-made explosive ever detonated. Its creator, nuclear physicist Andrei Sakharov, turned to political activism against proliferation of nuclear weapons. In 1975 he was awarded the Nobel Peace Prize for his anti-nuclear activism. He was banned from attending the ceremony, and exiled to a town far from Moscow.

[1] tandfonline.com/doi/pdf/10.2968/066004008.

The Cold War-Space Race

Throughout the 1960s, the Cold War dominated our lives on the ground and in the skies. Cold War tensions affected everything from our politics and education, to our interests in fashion and popular culture. In 1961, the USSR achieved many firsts in the Space Race, putting them at a military, technological and intellectual advantage.

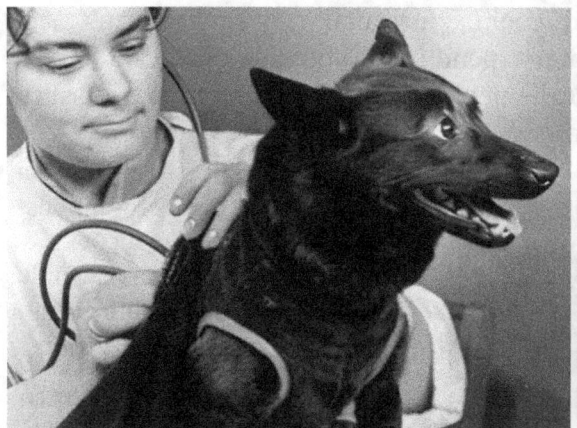

Chernushka during a pre-flight checkup.

Cosmonaut Yuri Gagarin.

A dog named Chernushka, some mice and a guinea pig launched into low earth orbit aboard the Soviet's Korabl-Sputnik 4 on 9th March 1961. They completed one orbit, landing safely after 88.6 minutes.

One month later cosmonaut Yuri Gagarin became the first human in space, circling the earth once in a 108-minute orbital flight on 12th April 1961, aboard Vostok 1.

Cosmonaut Gherman Titov became the second human to orbit earth, when Vostok 2 launched on 6th Aug 1961, orbiting 17 times over 25 hours, 18 minutes.

Valentina Tereshkova, first woman in space on 16th June 1963.

Alexei Leonov, first person to walk in space on 18th March 1965.

Throughout the decade the USSR continued to lead the Space Race with longer space flights, more complex space walks and other technical activities performed while in orbit.

Alan Shepard, 5th May 1961.

The Soviet's success with Gagarin was a blow to the Americans, who had hoped to be the first to send a man to space.

After repeated technical delays, astronaut Alan Shepard had the bittersweet honor of being the second man (first American) in space on 5th May 1961. NASA's vastly inferior Mercury-Redstone 3 brought him for a short, 15-minute suborbital trajectory before falling back to earth.

NASA sent a second American to space on 21st July 1961, when Mercury-Redstone 4 brought Virgil Grissom for a similar 15-minute suborbital trajectory.

NASA's first full orbit of earth with a man on board occurred in 1962, nearly a full year behind the Soviets. Between 1961 and 1963, the six Mercury Program missions primarily focused on orbiting the earth.

1961 also saw the commencement of two new space programs:

– The Gemini Program (1961-1966), focused on training and practice of space activities.

– The Apollo Program (1961-1972), with the aim of landing humans on the moon.

NASA astronauts Neil Armstrong and Edwin "Buzz" Aldrin took part in both Gemini and Apollo missions.

The USA would achieve its goal, winning the Space Race in 1969 when Apollo 11 brought Armstrong and Aldrin to the moon for their historic lunar walk, lasting $2^1/_4$ hours.

Buzz Aldrin walks on the moon. Photo by Neil Armstrong on 20th July 1969.

Space Race Inspired Movies — Advertisements

Poster for *Battle of the Worlds*, 1961.

Poster for *The Phantom Planet*, 1961.

As the Cold War turned our attention skywards, movies about space travel or alien invasions gained in popularity.

Poster for *Nude on the Moon*, 1961.

Poster for *Invasion of the Neptune Men*, 1961.

Cuba Invasion at Bay of Pigs

17th–19th April 1961

On 17th April 1961, 1,400 Cuban exiles landed at the Bay of Pigs on Cuba's south coast, in a brazen attempt to topple the communist military dictatorship of Fidel Castro. The failed US-backed attack saw almost 1,200 members of the exile invasion force captured and imprisoned.

Fidel Castro in 1961.

Members of the Cuban-exile invasion force, known as Brigade 2506, captured by the Cuban military and imprisoned.

Air strikes had been scheduled to disable Cuban Air Force bases prior to the surprise beach invasion. American bombers missed most of the Cuban targets. The unharmed Cuban Air Force swiftly attacked the invasion army, their escort ships and the US air support.

The invasion was supported by the CIA, who trained the exiles in combat techniques throughout 1960. Their secret training camps in Guatemala soon became common knowledge, receiving regular press coverage and compromising the surprise element of the attack.

The prisoners of the Bay of Pigs invasion remained in captivity for 20 months while President Kennedy negotiated a release deal. In December 1962, all the prisoners were brought home to the US in exchange for $53 million worth of baby food and medicine. Their return occurred just two months after the end of the Cuban Missile Crisis.

President Kennedy and Jacqueline Kennedy greet returned prisoners from Cuba, 29th December 1962.

Berlin Builds a Wall

13th August 1961

On 13th August 1961, the communist government of East Germany commenced building a fortified wall to surround West Berlin. 200 km (124 miles) of barbed wire entanglements were laid overnight. Within a few days, construction began on the permanent reinforced concrete wall.

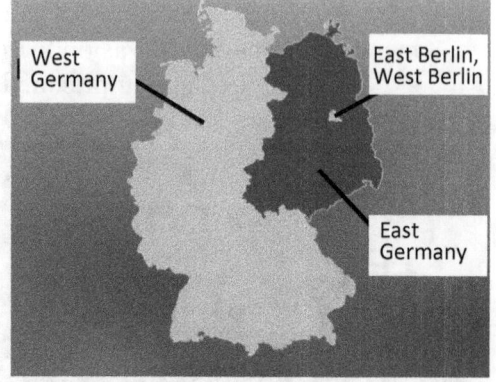

The aim of the Berlin Wall was to prevent East Germans from fleeing to the West, via the transport corridor from West Berlin to West Germany. A total of 3.5 million East Germans had defected since the end of WWII.

In 1962 a second parallel wall was constructed to create an open space of no-man's land, patrolled by tanks and soldiers. 116 watchtowers were manned 24 hours a day by armed guards instructed to kill any defectors.

East German construction workers building the Berlin Wall, 20th November 1961.

The wall did not wholly prevent the flood of defectors. From 1961 until the wall came down in 1989, at least 5,000 East Germans successfully escaped to the West. 170 or more were killed in their attempt.

On 9th November 1989, the Berlin Wall opened its borders and was dismantled. East and West Germany reunited as one country the following year.

Crowds at the Brandenburg Gate after the opening of the Berlin Wall, 1st December 1989.

The Cold War-Battlefield Vietnam

Fearful that a "domino effect" would see an uncontained spread of communism across the world, the US committed to supporting South Vietnam, financially and militarily, during its 30-year-long bloody civil war against North Vietnam (the Viet Cong). At the same time, communist China and USSR were jointly aiding the Viet Cong's invasion southward. Vietnam had become a Cold War battlefield.

America's involvement in the Vietnam War (known in Vietnam as the American War) intensified in May 1961 when President Kennedy ordered 400 American Green Beret Special Advisors to be sent to train the South Vietnamese soldiers in combat methods.

US Green Beret conducting training, 1961.

Under pressure from his military top brass to send American combat troops, President Kennedy resisted, instead sending additional military advisors in October 1961. A total of 16,000 were ultimately sent, along with American helicopters for transport use.

By the end of the year the US was spending a million dollars per day to support the South Vietnamese army.

President Kennedy continued to refuse the deployment of US combat troops in Vietnam. However, under the leadership of President Johnson in 1963, US combat troops began arriving by the thousands.

In all, 2.7 million American soldiers served in Vietnam over the ten years to 1973. More than 58,000 Americans died in battle, in addition to the more than 3 million Vietnamese (civilians and soldiers from both sides of battle).[1]

[1] britannica.com/event/Vietnam-War.

Advertisement

"Honest, Operator, I don't see any twenty on the clock!"

BELL TELEPHONE SYSTEM

"Honest, Operator, I don't see any twenty on the clock!"

Every five minutes the little boy would call and ask the same question... "Please, Operator, what time is it?"

But something about the little boy's voice told Operator Lola Caldwell that this was no childish prank. Finally, she asked him to call his mother to the phone.

"She can't come to the telephone," he said. "My baby sister swallowed a button this morning, and my mother had to take her to the hospital. And she told me not to dare leave the house till twenty after eight. I looked and looked, and honest, Operator, I don't see any twenty on the clock. And I'm afraid I'll miss my school bus."

"Don't worry, young man," said Mrs. Caldwell. "I'll call you when it's time to leave." At 8:20 she rang and sent the little boy off to meet his bus.

It's a true story, a small story–and to Lola Caldwell, all in the day's work. But it is typical of the personal interest that telephone people take in their customers.

Their desire to help makes them good neighbors in their own communities, keeps them on the job in fires, floods, blizzards. And in the process, you enjoy the best telephone service in the world.

Freedom Riders Against Segregation

4th May 1961

The first Freedom Rider's bus, firebombed in Anniston, Alabama, 14th May 1961.

On 4th May 1961, a group of six white and seven African American civil rights activists boarded a Greyhound bus in Washington D.C., with a plan to travel to New Orleans, Louisiana. Their aim was to highlight the unlawful continued segregation at bus facilities.

By using "whites-only" restrooms and lunch counters in racially divided southern states, the Freedom Riders were met with condemnation and violence from public and police.

Lewis[1] (top left) with the original Freedom Riders in 1961.

Arriving in Alabama, the bus was chased and set on fire. Several Riders were attacked by a violent mob of around 200 whites. Police had tipped-off Ku Klux Klan members to join the attack without fear of arrest. John Lewis,[1] one of the leaders, was among those attacked.

The second bus was also attacked by Klan members, armed with iron chains, bars, and baseball bats.

Throughout the summer, more than 60 Freedom Rides crossed the South, with beatings and arrests on such a large scale the jails were overflowing. Activists expanded their protests to include restaurants and hotels, forcing the larger chains to desegregate their businesses.

On 1st November 1961, the Interstate Commerce Commission ruled that passengers were permitted to sit and dine wherever they pleased. Racial segregation signs would finally be removed from all facilities.

---

[1] John Lewis, one of the original 13 Freedom Riders of 1961, was a life-long civil rights leader and politician. He was 1 of 6 organizers of the 1963 March on Washington. In 1965 he led the first of the Selma to Montgomery marches. A member of the Democratic Party, Lewis served 17 terms in the US House of Reps. from 1987 till his death in 2020.

Advertisement

This is New Woodhue—solid vinyl tile with the rich look and feel of fine parquet flooring!
The key to the smart woman's styling secret: coordination.
Congoleum-Nairn Vinyl Floors.

Imagine the beauty of this deep-grained Woodhue vinyl tile in your home! So easy to coordinate with furnishings. So like expensive wood parquet. You can actually feel the deep graining in new Woodhue by Congoleum-Nairn. Yet, in most 12' x 15' rooms, this lovely solid vinyl floor costs about $85—installed!

World Wildlife Fund Created   11th September 1961

In September 1961, a group of passionate conservationists from around the world came together to form the World Wildlife Fund (WWF), an organization dedicated to raising money necessary for the conservation and protection of threatened nature and wildlife species.

The WWF founders were motivated by the difficulties numerous well meaning conservation groups faced while raising money for their causes. As stated in the original manifesto of 1961, the WWF was committed to assisting worthy organizations struggling to save the world's wildlife.

Dutch Prince Bernhard of Lippe-Biesterfeld became the first President of the WWF, a position he held until 1976. Prince Philip, Duke of Edinburgh held the post from 1981-1996.

During the '60s, the WWF supported over 350 conservation projects around the world. Individual species and local habitats were focused on initially. Pandas, polar bears, black rhinos and the Galapagos Islands were some early selections for funding.

In more recent times, the WWF has aimed to raise awareness on global issues, focusing on sustainable development and the preservation of natural resources and biodiversity.

The WWF is now the World's largest conservation organization, with over 3,000 projects in more than 100 countries.

Advertisement

THE GLARING TRUTH ABOUT SUNGLASSES

WITHOUT POLAROID LENSES, ordinary sunglasses cut down light. They don't screen out the glare that really bothers your eyes—the reflected glare. Prove this for yourself with a three-second test at any nearby store where quality sunglasses are sold.

WITH POLAROID LENSES, Cool-Ray sunglasses stop the annoying—even painful —reflected glare. Cool-Ray† Polaroid® polarizing sunglasses screen out harmful ultraviolet rays, let only the gentle, useful light through. Accept no less for your only pair of eyes.

Smart new styles for men, women, and teenagers (and fit-ons to convert prescription glasses to Cool-Ray Polaroid Sunglasses), from $1.98, at your neighborhood stores (U.S. and Canada). Cool-Ray, Inc., 80 Heard Street, Boston 50, Mass.

® by Polaroid Corp.   †T.M. Reg. by Cool-Ray, Inc.

Make the 3-second test at your nearby store and prove to yourself that

Only Cool-Ray Polaroid Sunglasses stop reflected glare

The Glaring Truth About Sunglasses

Without Polaroid lenses, ordinary sunglasses cut down light. They don't screen out the glare that really bothers your eye—the reflected glare. Prove this for yourself with a three-second test at any nearby store where quality sunglasses are sold.

With Polaroid lenses, Cool-Ray sunglasses stop the annoying—even painful—reflected glare. Cool-Ray Polaroid polarizing sunglasses screen out harmful ultraviolet rays, let only the gentle, useful light through. Accept no less for your only pair of eyes.

Smart new styles for men, women, and teenagers (and fit-ons to convert prescription glasses to Cool-Ray Polaroid Sunglasses), from $1.98, at your neighborhood stores (U.S. and Canada). Cool-Ray, Inc...

Make the 3-second test at your nearby store and prove to yourself that

Only Cool-Ray Polaroid Sunglasses stop reflected glare

Advertisement

At Last...Prepared Dinners that are Really Different

Zesty, robust dinners anyone?

Here they are. Patio Mexican Style Dinners. Different? Exotically different. Enjoy savory *tamales,* choice tender beef rolled in genuine corn masa. A hearty beef *enchilada,* delicious meat center combined with a flavor-rich tortilla and garnished with Cheddar cheese. *Refritos,* luscious beans simmered slowly then whipped to bring out all their flavor goodness. Patio *Premium Chili,* selected beef and chili gravy seasoned to perfection. And a generous portion of long-grain *Spanish* rice. A complete dinner made according to traditional Mexican recipes, seasoned to please American tastes. And so simple to serve. Just heat... it's ready in minutes. For prepared dinners that are *really* different, get Patio Quick Frozen Mexican Style Dinners!

Your whole family will enjoy Patio Mexican Style Foods.

Enchilada Dinners · Beef Enchiladas · Chicken Enchiladas · Cheese Enchiladas · Tacos · Tortillas · Mexican Dinners

1961 in Cinema and Film

Charlton Heston as Rodrigo Diaz, leading a battle in the epic historical drama *El Cid*, 1961.

From its peak in the mid-1940s, cinema attendance faced a steady decline as television sets took pride of place in nearly every household. By 1961 many cinemas struggled to stay profitable and were forced to close. The motion picture industry needed to find ways to win over new audiences.

The rise of big budget epic films, such as *Ben Hur* (1959), *Spartacus* (1960), *El Cid* (1961), *King of Kings* (1961), and *The Guns of Navarone* (1961), took advantage of the new, bigger screen formats offered by VistaVision, Cinerama and Cinemascope, to lure back viewers. Extravagant and spectacular sets, exotic locations, multiple A-list actors and casts of thousands, ensured big ticket sales at the box office.

Warren Beatty in 1961.

1961 film debuts

Warren Beatty	Splendor in the Grass
Gene Hackman	Mad Dog Coll
Ron Howard	Five Minutes to Live
Dudley Moore	The Third Alibi
Mary Tyler Moore	X-15
Burt Reynolds	Angel Baby
George Segal	The Young Doctors

* From en.wikipedia.org/wiki/1961_in_film.

Top Grossing Films of the Year

1	West Side Story	Artists	$19,645,000
2	The Guns of Navarone	Columbia Pictures	$13,000,000
3	El Cid	Allied Artists	$12,000,000
4	The Parent Trap	Disney	$11,300,000
5	The Absent-Minded Professor	Disney	$11,100,000
6	Lover Come Back	Universal	$7,625,000
7	King of Kings	MGM	$6,520,000
8	One Hundred & One Dalmatians	Disney	$6,200,000
9	La Dolce Vita	Cineriz/Pathé	$6,000,000
10	Come September	Universal	$5,770,000

* From en.wikipedia.org/wiki/1961_in_film by box office gross in the USA.

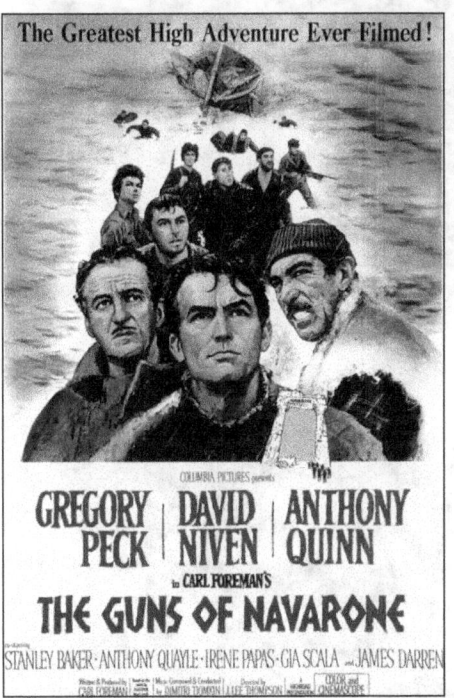

Based on Alistair MacLean's 1957 best selling novel, the big budget war epic *The Guns of Navarone* was filmed on location on the Greek Island of Rhodes.

One Hundred and One Dalmatians was Disney's 17th animated feature film.

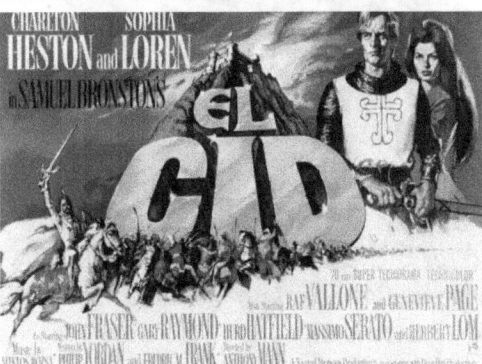

West Side Story Hits Cinemas   18ᵗʰ October 1961

Adapted from the hugely successful 1957 Broadway musical by Leonard Bernstein and Stephen Sondheim, the United Artists film version of *West Side Story* broke all box office records. It would be the highest grossing film of 1961 and win 10 of its 11 Academy Award nominations, a record for a musical film at the time.

Loosely based on the forbidden love story of Shakespeare's *Romeo and Juliet*, the musical tackles the darker themes of gang violence and racial tensions. With gritty sets and frequent use of common street slang, *West Side Story* was groundbreaking in the musical genre.

A young Natalie Wood was given the lead role of Maria, while Richard Beymer beat out Warren Beatty, Burt Reynolds, Richard Chamberlain and Robert Redford for the lead role of Tony. Both Wood and Beymer were accomplished actors but not strong singers, hence professional singers voiced all their songs in the movie.

The Gossip Magazines

Confidential, January 1961. *Inside Story,* May 1961.

Gossip or tabloid magazines flourished in the late '50s and early '60s. Focused on film and TV celebrities, their stories were substantially more explicit and provocative than the newspaper gossip columns.

Uncensored, October 1961. *Movie Life Yearbook,* 1961.

Advertisement

ALL THE FIXINGS FOR A HOMEMADE SPAGHETTI AND MEAT BALL DINNER

NEW!

SAUCE ALL MADE • 8 MEAT BALLS
QUICK-COOKING SPAGHETTI • LOTS OF GRATED CHEESE

Only Chef Boy-Ar-Dee has all you need to make a meal the way you like it.

You get complete sauce with the Chef's touch in it. Made from the finest ingredients, according to an old Italian recipe, carefully blended and slowly simmered. You get eight meaty meat balls. Big. Plump. Beefy. And spaghetti, eight full ounces to cook to taste. Spaghetti to make tender or firm—as you like it. And top off everything with the nippy Italian cheese that's aged just right. All for only pennies a serving.

Try Chef Boy-Ar-Dee Spaghetti Dinners with Meat or Mushroom Sauce.

Chef **BOY·AR·DEE**®
COMPLETE SPAGHETTI AND MEAT BALL DINNER

All the fixings for a homemade spaghetti and meat ball dinner
New! Sauce all made · 8 meatballs quick-cooking spaghetti · Lots of grated cheese
Only Chef Boy-Ar-Dee has all you need to make a meal the way you like it.
You get complete sauce with the Chef's touch in it. Made from the finest ingredients, according to an old Italian recipe, carefully blended and slowly simmered. You get eight meaty meat balls. Big. Plump. Beefy. And spaghetti, eight full ounces to cook to taste. Spaghetti to make tender or firm—as you like it. And top off everything with the nippy Italian cheese that's aged just right. All for only pennies a serving.
Try Chef Boy-Ah-Dee Spaghetti Dinners with Meat or Mushroom Sauce.
Chef Boy-Ah-Dee complete spaghetti and meat ball dinner

Advertisement

THINKING EUROPE?

Round-trip Chicago-Rome **ONLY $555**
Chicago-Copenhagen Round-trip **$497 ONLY**
Round-trip Chicago-Paris **ONLY $461**
Chicago-London **ONLY $421**
Detroit-Vienna **ONLY $514**
Lisbon **$433**
Round-trip Detroit-Frankfurt **ONLY $473**

17-day Economy Excursion fares by Pan Am Jet, effective October 1st through March 31st.

Now—*two* can fly abroad on Pan Am Jet Economy fares—for the price of *one* first-class ticket

Enjoy Europe's Open House this Autumn, just when Pan Am Jet fares are at their lowest....

Gone are the tourist crowds from hotels, shops and restaurants. Festivals begin. People relax. The welcome becomes just a bit more personal. No wonder the experienced traveler chooses these off-season months to see the real Europe, and chooses Pan Am to see more of it—more pleasantly. You can save up to $136 over regular economy fares. And the fares listed above are just a few tempting samples of Pan Am bargains in off-season travel.

You can fly giant Pan Am Jet Clippers* direct from any of 11 U.S. Gateway cities to Europe. Pan Am offers the widest choice of Jet flights—49 a week—and Pan Am Jets fly direct to 20 major European cities, far more than any other airline. See your Travel Agent, and insist on Pan Am, the airline that adds the Priceless Extra of Experience to every flight.

WORLD'S MOST EXPERIENCED AIRLINE—FIRST ON THE ATLANTIC...FIRST ON THE PACIFIC...FIRST IN LATIN AMERICA...FIRST 'ROUND THE WORLD

Thinking Europe? Now—*two* can fly abroad on Pan Am Jet Economy fares —for the price of *one* first-class ticket.

Enjoy Europe's Open House this Autumn, just when Pan Am Jet fares are at their lowest...

Gone are the tourist crowds from hotels, shops and restaurants. Festivals begin. People relax. The welcome becomes just a bit more personal. No wonder the experienced traveler chooses these off-season months to see the real Europe, and chooses Pan Am to see more of it—more pleasantly. You can save up to $136 over regular economy fares. And the fares listed above are just a few tempting samples of Pan Am bargains in off-season travel.

You can fly giant Pan Am Jet Clippers direct from any of 11 U.S. Gateway cities to Europe. Pan Am offers the widest choice of jet flights—49 a week—and Pan Am Jets fly direct to 20 major European cities, far more than any other airline. See your Travel Agent, and insist on Pan Am, the airline that adds the Priceless Extra of Experience to every flight.

World's most experienced airline—first on the Atlantic... first on the Pacific... first in Latin America... first 'round the world.

Who Were The Rat Pack?

They were known as The Rat Pack—a group of entertainer friends, who sang together, acted together, played hard and drank harder together. They had links to politicians, mafia, and Hollywood elite. In the early '60s, their favorite hangout was The Sands Hotel in Las Vegas, and between them, they transformed this dusty, desert town into the glamorous gambling and entertainment capitol of the world.

At its core, the Pack comprised: Frank Sinatra, Dean Martin, Sammy Davis Jnr, Peter Lawford and Joey Bishop. Their shows were broadcast on live TV, enticing other celebrities to perform in Las Vegas, turning it into a tourist destination town.

The Rat Pack were the kings of cool. They had swag, talent, energy, money and power. To see the Rat Pack at the Sands, a show with dinner and two drinks, cost a cool $5.95 per person.

At their peak, The Rat Pack made 5 films together including *Ocean's 11* (Warner Bros. 1960), *Sergeants Three* (United Artists, 1962), and *Four for Texas* (Warner Bros. 1963).

Below Left: Martin, Judy Garland & Sinatra.
Below Right: Sinatra, the leader of The Pack, recorded 14 albums during the years 1961 to 1963.

Musical Memories

American style rock 'n' roll ruled the decade of the 1950s, with Elvis as its king. Worldwide, movies, television, fashion, youth culture and attitudes had been influenced by this American export. But by the start of 1961, British home-grown rock artists were developing their own unique interpretation of the rock genre. And within a short few years, their international success–known as the British Invasion– would make The Beatles, Cliff Richard, The Kinks, The Who, The Rolling Stones, The Yardbirds, and others, household names.

15th Jan– Motown Records signed The Supremes, an all-girl group who would become the most successful of Motown's acts.

29th April– Luciano Pavarotti made his debut as Rodolfo in *La Bohème* at the Teatro Municipale (Reggio Emilia).

23rd Apr-21st May– Judy Garland performed a series of much anticipated concerts at Carnegie Hall.

The Country Music Hall of Fame was formed in 1961, inducting Jimmie Rodgers, Fred Rose and Hank Williams as its first three members.

January– The Beatles commenced live performances in and around Liverpool, UK. It would be another two years, with final "Fab Four", manager and record label in place, before they would make their first recording at EMI's Abbey Road Studios.

1961 Billboard Top 30 Songs

	Artist	Song Title
1	Bobby Lewis	Tossin' and Turnin'
2	Patsy Cline	I Fall to Pieces
3	The Highwaymen	Michael
4	Roy Orbison	Crying
5	Del Shannon	Runaway
6	The Jive Five	My True Story
7	Chubby Checker	Pony Time
8	The String-A-Longs	Wheels
9	Dee Clark	Raindrops
10	Joe Dowell	Wooden Heart

Patsy Cline, 1957.

Chubby Checker, 1964.

Roy Orbison, 1965.   Del Shannon, 1965.

Artist	Song Title
11 Lawrence Welk	Calcutta
12 Bobby Vee	Take Good Care of My Baby
13 Roy Orbison	Running Scared
14 The Shirelles	Dedicated to the One I Love
15 The Mar-Keys	Last Night
16 The Shirelles	Will You Love Me Tomorrow
17 Ferrante & Teicher	Exodus
18 Connie Francis	Where the Boys Are
19 Ray Charles	Hit the Road Jack
20 Sue Thompson	Sad Movies (Make Me Cry)

Connie Francis, 1961.

The Shirelles, 1962.

21 Ernie K-Doe	Mother-in-Law
22 The Dovells	Bristol Stomp
23 Ricky Nelson	Travelin' Man
24 The Miracles	Shop Around
25 Brook Benton	The Boll Weevil Song
26 Gene McDaniels	A Hundred Pounds of Clay
27 Dick and Dee Dee	The Mountain's High
28 Marty Robbins	Don't Worry
29 Floyd Cramer	On the Rebound
30 Steve Lawrence	Portrait of My Love

* From the *Billboard* top 30 singles of 1961.

Advertisement

Dresses from the *Lana Lobell Spring Home Shopping Catalog*, 1961.

Fashion Trends of the 1960s

The 1960s was a decade of fashion extremes driven by a vibrant and vocal youth, shifting social movements, rebelliousness and rejection of traditions. It was an exciting decade for fashion, with new trends that caught on and shifted quickly.

In the early '60s, fashion was content to continue the conservative classic style of the previous decade. The elegant sheath dress and tailored skirt-suits were still favored for day wear. And no lady would dare to venture out without her full ensemble of matching accessories. Gloves, hat, scarf, jewelry and stiletto or kitten-heel shoes were mandatory for any outing.

Christian Dior's voluptuous "New Look", favored throughout the 1950s, was still popular for cocktails or dinners. Less formal than the stiffer '50s styles, dresses retained their hour-glass shape but were now made with softer patterned fabrics. Skirts stayed long, full and very lady-like.

Television, cinema and magazine coverage kept us abreast of the latest in haute couture and street style, inspiring us with our favorite fashion icons.

Jacqueline Kennedy may have been the US first lady for only three years, but as first lady of fashion, her iconic status has endured till this day.

Jacqueline Kennedy, wearing her signature pearl necklace.

Always impeccably groomed, with perfectly applied make-up and coiffured hair, here are a few of her iconic looks:

- Tailored skirt-suit with three-quarter-sleeve box jacket and pill box hat in matching fabric.
- Sheath dress, low-heeled pump shoes and three-quarter gloves.
- A-line dress, long or short, with long gloves for evening.

After more than a decade of adherence to Dior's New Look, the first rumblings of change were being felt from Europe. The fashion houses of Italy were enticing us with bold new shapes and modern textiles.

Laminated silk shirt with elastic jersey pants by Emilio Schuberth. Layered form dress by Cesare Guidi.

Advertisement

Avon introduces Lipstick Deluxe

Outside news! Case on a golden base...a shimmering silvery cap, crowned with a sparkling jewel-like appliqué.

Inside news! The lipstick itself—so creamy, comfortable! Clings for hours, keeps its clear outline. All you've wished for in a lipstick! And there blooms a new shade too. Rose Gay, rosiest pink ever!

"Avon calling" to show you this magnificent new lipstick, and offer you a miniature gift in the shade of your choice.

Avon cosmetics
New York • Montreal
75 years of beauty service to the home

Advertisement

How sugar helps the weight you lose stay lost

For many people the real weight control problem begins when a reducing diet ends

With the bars down, your appetite is ready to go on a spree

Sugar can help make your appetite behave. A little sugar satisfies faster than a lot of other foods

That's why most weight-watcher diets include sugar and foods containing sugar

Why mountain climbers carry sugar. A 15-minute climb can drain more energy than a 5-mile walk. That's why mountain climbers tuck sugar or snacks containing sugar in their knapsacks. Sugar is one of Nature's best answers to your need for quick energy—whether you're scaling a mountain or just a flight of stairs.

Why do they put sugar in the pickle jar? It's not just to sweeten the pickles. Recent experiments show that sugar brings out the natural flavor. Pickles taste "picklier," fruit tastes "fruitier," even soup tastes brighter. Next time you make vegetable soup, add a little sugar and see for yourself.

18 CALORIES! Surprise you that there are only 18 calories in a teaspoonful of sugar? (Some people have guessed as high as 600.)

Sugar satisfies your appetite faster—and with fewer calories—than most other foods.

All statements in this message apply to both beet and cane sugar.

Published in the interest of better nutrition by **SUGAR INFORMATION, INC.** a non-profit organization

The decade of the 1960s would belong to the British youth centered around London, who would soon capture the world's attention with their free spirits, energy, music, and style. The "British Invasion" exploded onto the world in the early '60s, introducing us to the "Mods", and later to the "Swinging Sixties". These movements defined the era and changed the world of fashion forever.

The Mods were clean-cut college boys who favored slim-fitting suits or short jackets over turtle-neck or buttoned up polo shirts. Pants were pipe-legged with no cuffs, worn over pointed polished shoes or ankle boots. Mods were obsessed with Italian fashion, French haircuts, and alternative music.

For the girls, London designer Mary Quant created fashion for the young and free-spirited woman. Quant invented the mini skirt, worn with bold colored or patterned tights. Her boutique featured simple short dresses in bold or floral patterns.

By the mid- '60s, Quant championed hot pants for women. Her experimental use of new materials was revolutionary. She created synthetic dresses, patent plastic boots, shiny PVC raincoats and bold colorful jewelry, handbags and accessories.

By the mid-'60s the world would be captivated by the unstoppable energy of London's Swinging Sixties. The term captured the modern fun-loving hedonism of swinging London. It was the era of the British supermodel—tall, skinny, leggy young ladies, with enormous eyes and descriptive names. Jean Shrimpton, Twiggy, and Penelope Tree were in-demand icons world-wide. The British supermodels broke with the aristocratic look of earlier-generation models, redefining beauty standards for a younger, more care-free generation.

Penelope Tree for *Vogue*, October 1967.

Twiggy for *Italian Vogue*, July 1967.

Twiggy various photo shoots.

Jean Shrimpton for *Australian Women's Weekly*, August 1965.

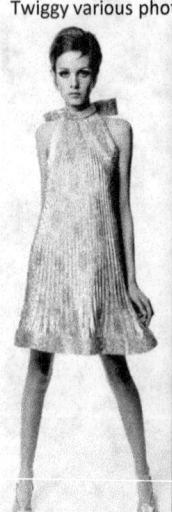

As the fashion and attitudes of swinging London spread to America and other parts of the world, the sub-culture became commercialized on a mass scale and began to loose its vitality. The Swinging Sixties morphed into the psychedelic rock and early hippie movements.

Led by musicians such as The Beatles, The Beach Boys, Pink Floyd and The Who, and fuelled by the widespread use of marijuana and LSD, psychedelic fashion became an expression of the hallucinogenic experience with bright colors, swirling patterns and kaleidoscopic floral designs.

From The Beatles *Magical Mystery Tour,* 1967.

The psychedelic rock movement petered out by the end of the 1960s, but the hippie generation was only just beginning. Hippies would drive fashion forward, well into the next decade.

Take your child out of the crowd with the 1961 World Book Encyclopedia

Naturally, you want your child to stand out—to be better than vaguely "average." One of the best ways you can help is by providing the advantage of World Book Encyclopedia in your home. World Book *helps bring out the best* in any student, actually helps increase his chances for success. More than any other encyclopedia, World Book is *planned* for the home as well as school. It is easy to use, inviting to read, and its articles are clearly explained and made memorable with the help of 22,000 illustrations–5,000 of them in full, rich color. If you want your child to have the best in life, give him the finest in home education help... *World Book Encyclopedia!*

First in Sales... Quality... Leadership!
Aristocratic binding. 24K gold stamping and top edge gilding. 20 volumes... $179 (other bindings lower). Easy terms $10 down... $6 a month.

Save $49! Order the enlarged 1961 Childcraft with World Book Encyclopedia.
A $298 value. Both for only $249. Jus $10 down, $10 a month.

Childcraft... Internationally Famous Child Development Plan... is a 15-volume treasury of knowledge for younger children, filled with fun and carefully-planned instructional helps that give a memorable background for school and for life. Includes guidance volumes for parents.

Advertisement

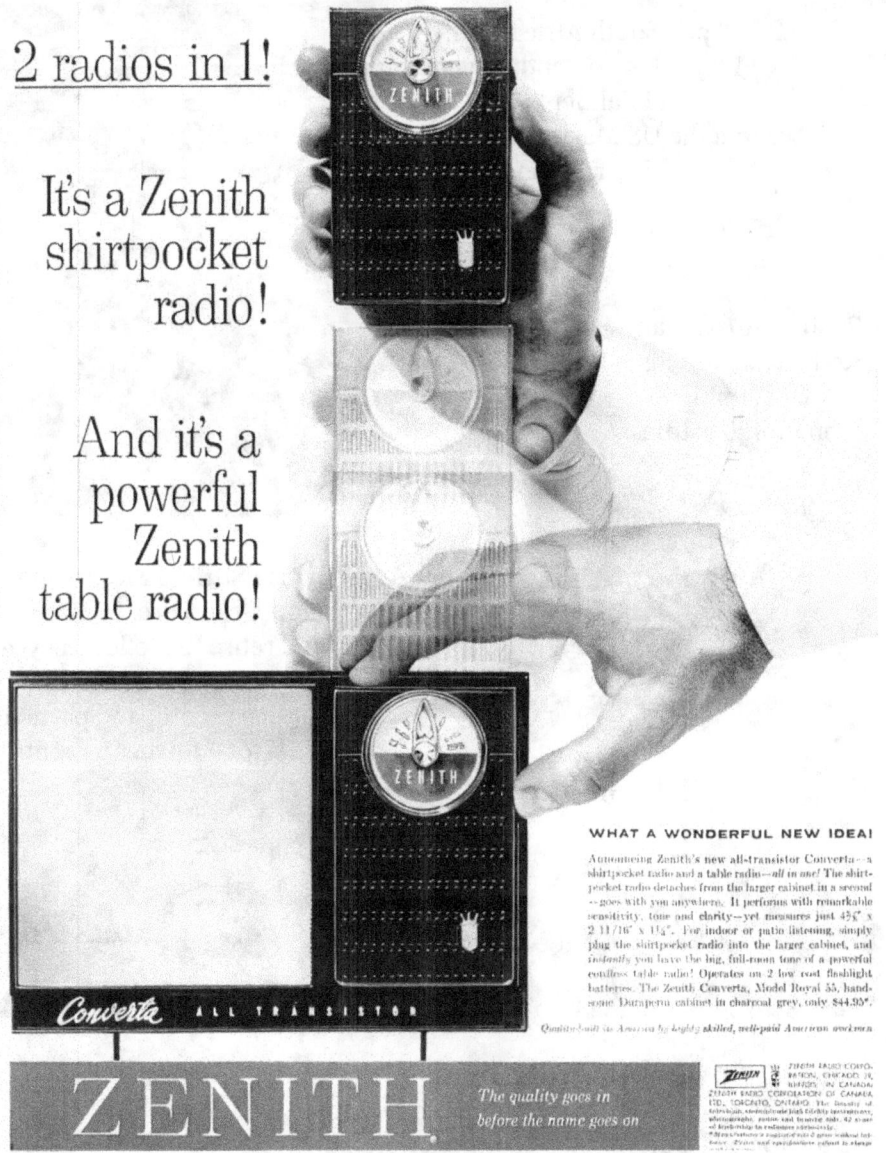

2 radios in 1! It's a Zenith shirtpocket radio! And it's a powerful Zenith table radio! What a wonderful new idea!

Announcing Zenith's new all-transistor Converta—a shirtpocket radio and a table radio—*all in one!* The shirtpocket radio detaches from the larger cabinet in a second—goes with you anywhere. It performs with remarkable sensitivity, tone and clarity—yet measures just $4^3/_8$" x $2^{11}/_{16}$" x $1^1/_4$". For indoor or patio listening, simply plug the shirtpocket radio into the larger cabinet, and *instantly* you have the big, full-room tone of a powerful cordless table radio! Operates on 2 low cost flashlight batteries. The Zenith Converta, Model Royal 55, handsome Duraperm cabinet in charcoal grey, only $44.95.

Quality-built in America by highly skilled, well-paid American workmen.

Also in Sports

25th Apr– South African golfer Gary Player beat defending champion Arnold Palmer by one stroke to become the US Masters Tournaments first international Champion.

7th Jul– Australian Rod Laver won his 1st of 4 Wimbledon Men's Singles titles.

6th Aug– British Stirling Moss won his 16th Formula 1 Grand Prix in Monaco. He would retire the following year after a crash at Goodwood left him in a coma for one month, and partially paralyzed for a further 6 months.

10th Sep– Tragedy at the Italian Grand Prix race at Monza when Baron Wolfgang von Trips crashed his Ferrari into an embankment filled with spectators. The driver plus 13 others were killed.

1st Oct– Roger Maris for baseball's New York Yankees hit 61 home runs for the 1961 Major League season, breaking Babe Ruth's 34-year record.

19th Nov– Gordie Howe became the 1st player to play in 1,000 National Hockey League (NHL) games.

3rd Dec– Dutchman Anton Geesink became the first non-Japanese judo world champion.

Science and Medicine

19th May– The Soviet's Venera 1 space probe became the first craft from Earth to fly past Venus. Launched in Feb 1961, the unmanned probe lost contact with Earth, rendering it unable to transmit data during its fly-past.

19th Jul– TWA became the first airline to offer in-flight movies. *By Love Possessed* (United Artists, 1961) starring Lana Turner was shown on a New York to Los Angeles flight to first class passengers.

31st Jul– IBM introduced the "golf ball" Selectric typewriter, replacing individual keys on separate swinging arms with a rotating ball containing all the letters and special characters. Selectrics eventually captured 75% of the typewriter market.

The drug Diazepam (also known as Valium) was developed in 1961 by research chemists L. H. Sternbach and E. Reeder for Hoffmann-La Roche. Patented and launched in 1963, the drug became one of the world's most frequently prescribed medicines, commonly taken for its calming effects to aid with insomnia, depression, and anxiety. Popularly referred to as "mother's little helper", the drug has since been proven to cause substance dependance and abuse when combined with alcohol or drugs or taken recreationally in excessive quantities.

Joseph Engelberger, known as the Father of Robotics, created his "Unimate" prototype for General Motors in 1959. By 1961, his "Unimate 1900" became the first mass produced robotic arm. It was employed to do tasks deemed too dangerous for humans, such as diecasting in the General Motors' assembly line.

Other News from 1961

1st Jan– The farthing coin (worth $1/4$ of a penny), ceased to be legal tender in the United Kingdom. The farthing had been in use since the 13th century.

28th May– Amnesty International was founded in London, UK, as an NGO focused on exposing human rights violations worldwide and providing legal assistance to political prisoners. It is currently active in more than 150 nations.

30th May– Dominican dictator Rafael Trujillo was assassinated. Nicknamed "El Jefe" (the boss), Trujillo had ruled for 31 brutal years.

23rd Jun– The Antarctic Treaty System was adopted, regulating international relations with respect to Antarctica. The Treaty ensured that Antarctica would be preserved for peaceful research and the promotion of international scientific cooperation.

30th Jun– The newly independent nation of Kuwait requested British military assistance and protection, fearing threats of occupation from neighboring Iraq. Within days the UK had sent military land, sea and air forces. Iraq did not attack.

2nd Jul– Novelist and journalist Ernest Hemmingway (aged 61) was found dead from a self-inflicted gunshot wound. Hemmingway is remembered as one of America's greatest 20th century novelists, having won the Pulitzer Prize in 1953, and the Nobel Prize in Literature in 1954.

July– Luxury fashion house Yves Saint Laurent was founded in Paris by business partners Yves Saint Laurent and Pierre Bergé.

10th Oct– A volcanic eruption on the island of Tristan da Cunha in the South Atlantic Sea resulted in the island's entire population being evacuated. As a British Overseas Territory, the Islanders were brought to Surrey in the UK for resettlement until it was safe to return home. Most of the Islanders returned in 1963.

1st Nov– 50,000 women, representing the newly formed activist group Women Strike for Peace, marched in 60 cities across the US to demonstrate against nuclear weapons. Such marches were uncommon at the time, paving the way for future anti-Vietnam War marches of the late '60s.

6th Nov– The United Nations General Assembly formally condemned South Africa's racist Apartheid policies, calling on member nations to end economic and military relations with the country.

19th Dec– After 451 years of Portuguese rule, the Governor General of Portugal in Goa signed a document of surrender delivering Goa, Daman and Diu to the rule of India. The surrender came after 2 days of continuous land, sea and air strikes by the Indian Armed Forces.

1961– Proctor & Gamble introduced the Pampers disposable diaper.

Advertisement

- Now–no darkroom needed to develop picture after picture with amazing new Rollaprint • New–make one print or 100 from your favorite negatives in normal room light with amazing Rollaprint • You–make permanent pictures–in less than 10 seconds for less than 5 cents with amazing new Rollaprint • For the first time give an entirely new gift for father's day, graduates, too! Only $19.95

You don't need a darkroom! So easy, that even a child can do it; here's how:
• All popular size negatives. Various masks are included to provide attractive, professional white borders on all prints up to $3^1/_4$" x $4^1/_4$". • Exposure in seconds. Rollaprint paper is exposed quickly in light box. Prints made in normal room light. Now, no darkroom needed! • Pictures develop quickly. Insert exposed Rollaprint paper in slot, turn crank evenly. Chemicals develop & fix pictures permanently.
• Finished prints in seconds. From start to finish, perfect prints in less than 10 seconds, for less than 5 cents each. Make as many as you like!

Rollaprint paper, 100 sheets, $2.95; Rollaprint chemicals, set $1.95.

Introducing! The sensational new Rollaprint 35mm Enlarger. Only $37.50. Enlarge your favorite 35mm negatives to permanent $3^1/_4$" x $4^1/_4$" prints, without a darkroom, in less than 10 seconds, for less than 5 cents!

Advertisement

you what? you forgot to bring the beer?

Pity the poor crew that sets sail without the beer. Better to have forgotten the anchor? Beer really belongs on a day like this. Can you imagine... water, water everywhere and not a drop of beer to drink? For that matter, is there *any* warm weather activity that doesn't call for a tall, cool satisfying glass of good beer or ale? Now, don't *you* go forgetting the beer on your next outing. Guests have been known to mutiny, you know.

The United States Brewers Association, inc.
...whose members make today's finest beer and ale.

On a bright summer day: Nothing else is as good as a good glass of beer.

Famous People Born in 1961

13th Jan– Julia Louis-Dreyfus, American actress & comedienne.

10th Feb– George Stephanopoulos, American political commentator, advisor & journalist.

4th Mar– Ray "Boom Boom" Mancini, American boxer.

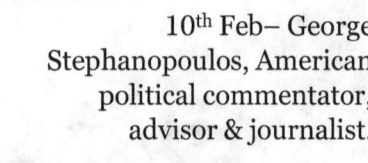

17th Mar– Dana Reeve, American actress & activist (Christopher & Dana Reeve Foundation).

3rd Apr– Eddie Murphy, American actor.

12th Apr– Magda Szubanski, Australian actress.

14th Apr– Robert Carlyle, British actor.

26th Apr– Joan Chen [Chen Chong], Chinese-American actress.

1st May– Steven Cauthen, American Hall of Fame jockey.

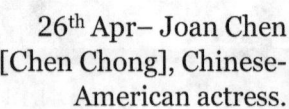

6th May– George Clooney, American actor.

8th May– Bill de Blasio, American politician & NYC Mayor (2013-).

13th May– Dennis Rodman, NBA forward (Chicago Bulls).

17th May– Enya (Eithne Ní Bhraonáin), Irish singer & songwriter.

26th May– Stephen Pate, American golfer (6 PGA Tour titles).

29th May– Melissa Etheridge, American singer, songwriter & guitarist.

1st Jun– Paul Coffey, Canadian hockey defense (Hockey Hall of Fame).

9th Jun– Michael J. Fox, Canadian actor, author, comedian & activist.

14th Jun– Boy George (Alan O'Dowd), British singer-songwriter.

18th Jun– Alison (Genevieve) Moyet, English rock vocalist.

25th Jun– Ricky Gervais, English actor & comedian.

1st Jul– Diana Spencer, Princess of Wales, England (d. 1997).

1st Jul– Carl Lewis, American sprinter & long jumper.

15th Jul– Forest Whitaker, American actor & director.

23rd Jul– Woody Harrelson, American actor.

1st Aug– Brad Faxon Jr, American golfer (8 PGA Tour titles).

4th Aug– Barack Obama, 44th USA President (Democrat: 2009-2017).

25th Aug– Billy Ray Cyrus, American country singer.

27th Aug– Tom Ford, American fashion designer.

25th Sep– Heather Locklear, American actress.

29th Sep– Julia Gillard, Australian politician, 1st female Prime Minister (2010-2013).

31st Oct– Peter Jackson, New Zealand film director.

19th Nov– Meg Ryan, American actress.

24th Nov– Arundhati Roy, Indian activist & writer.

Advertisement

100 ft. roll wraps 100 sandwiches yet sells at wax paper prices!

Clear new Handi-Wrap keeps sandwiches fresh up to 3 times longer than ordinary sandwich wrap—now you can make sandwiches the night before! Handi-Wrap won't leak, stays put, yet it's so easy to handle. And you get 100 feet at wax paper prices!

1961 in Numbers

Census Statistics [1]

- Population of the world   3.09 billion
- Population in the United States   189.57 million
- Population in the United Kingdom   52.72 million
- Population in Canada   18.23 million
- Population in Australia   10.45 million
- Average age for marriage of women   20.3 years old
- Average age for marriage of men   22.8 years old
- Average family income USA $5,700 per year
- Minimum wage USA $1.15 per hour

Costs of Goods [2]

- Average home — $19,365
- Average new car — $2,850
- New Pontiac Bonneville — $3,255
- A gallon of gasoline — $0.31
- Apples — $0.29 per 3 pounds
- A loaf of bread — $0.25
- A gallon of milk — $1.00
- Sirloin steak — $0.89 per pound
- Lamb chops — $0.59 per pound
- Sliced bacon — $0.67 per pound
- Fresh Eggs — $0.57 per dozen
- McDonald's hamburger — $0.15
- Swanson chicken TV dinner — $0.49
- A cinema ticket — $0.77

---

[1] Figures taken from worldometers.info/world-population, US National Center for Health Statistics, Divorce and Divorce Rates US (cdc.gov/nchs/data/series/sr_21/sr21_029.pdf) and US Census Bureau, Historical Marital Status Tables (census.gov/data/tables/time-series/demo/families/marital.html).
[2] From thepeoplehistory.com, mclib.info/reference/local-history & dqydj.com/historical-home-prices/.

Advertisement

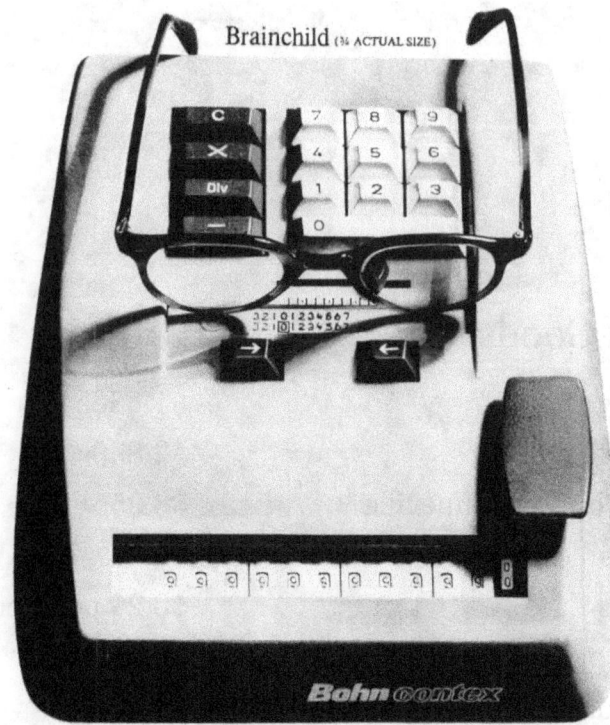

"$125! How good can it be?"

Bohn Contex Calculator

"$125! How good can it be?"

You can't blame a businessman who pays $500 to $1,000 for an office calculator for being skeptical about what he can get for $125. And for looking twice at our Brainchild that claims to do just about everything the big, expensive machines do...and a couple of things they can't. The big machines add, subtract, multiply and divide. So does the Bohn Contex.

The expensive machines give a running total, include and automatic decimal indicator and hold a constant. So does the Bohn Contex.

Now here's what the big calculators can't do. They can't double as high-speed 10-key adding-subtracting machines. The Bohn Contex can. They can't be operated by anyone after just a few minutes instruction. The Bohn Contex can.

Most important of all, the Bohn Contex is the first compact, 10-key calculator that's truly portable. Brainchild of top international designers, it weighs only six pounds and is no bigger than your telephone. Slips into a briefcase and goes to work anywhere. Executive office, accounting department, out in the field, on business trips, plane, train, home...anywhere. Businessmen, salesmen, engineers, architects, students, housewives find the Bohn Contex the easiest, fastest way to figure bills, invoices, percentages, extensions, estimates, income tax... All this for only $125! No wonder they were skeptical.

Advertisement

"Me earn $300,000?"

That's right. You can expect to earn $300,000 during your lifetime–provided you get some kind of special training. Where to get the training that's best for you? Get a college education if you can–but if you can't, we suggest the Army.

Why the Army? Because the Army, like a good college, offers a plus. The Army offers the finest of technical training–plus leadership training second to none.

And here's an important point: the Army lets you choose exactly the training that's right for you, before you enlist. You can pick your technical training from more than 100 courses. If you're not absolutely sure of what you want, the Army's tests will help you make up your mind on the basis of your suitability. In any case, whatever course you select, the Army guarantees you'll get what you choose–provided you've qualified in advance, of course. Remember: you can take qualifying tests before you enlist...choose your training before you enlist...and you're under no obligation to enlist!

You'll go a long way before you get a better offer. We suggest you look into it now. See your Army Recruiter while quotas are still open.

These words first appeared in print in the year 1961.

- HOLIDAYS
- Black Friday
- Affirmative Action
- Antidepressant
- highflier
- LOW EARTH ORBIT
- mind-altering
- Operating system
- photo-realism
- Computer science
- Eating disorder
- BIONIC
- multigenerational
- surf and turf
- FIBER-OPTIC
- TOASTER OVEN
- AA Battery

*From merriam-webster.com/time-traveler/1961.

A heartfelt plea from the author:

I sincerely hope you enjoyed reading this book and that it brought back many fond memories from the past.

Success as an author has become increasingly difficult with the proliferation of **AI generated** copycat books by unscrupulous sellers. They are clever enough to escape copyright action and use dark web tactics to secure paid-for **fake reviews**, something I would never do.

Hence I would like to ask you—I plead with you—the reader, to leave a star rating or review on Amazon. This helps make my book discoverable for new readers, and helps me to compete fairly against the devious copycats.

If this book was a gift to you, you can leave stars or a review on your own Amazon account, or you can ask the gift-giver or a family member to do this on your behalf.

I have enjoyed researching and writing this book for you and would greatly appreciate your feedback.

Best regards,
Bernard Bradforsand-Tyler.

Please leave a
book review/rating at:

https://bit.ly/1961-reviews

Or scan the QR code:

Flashback books make the perfect gift-

see the full range at

https://bit.ly/FlashbackSeries

Image Attributions

Photographs and images used in this book are reproduced courtesy of the following:

Page 6 – 1961 Sears: Tower Automatic 127. Source: flickr.com/photos/nesster/5917603945/ by Nesster. Attribution 4.0 (Creative Commons (CC) BY 4.0).
Page 8 – Source: envisioningtheamericandream.com. Pre 1978, no copyright mark. (PD image).
Page 9 – Source: envisioningtheamericandream.com. Pre 1978, no copyright mark (PD image).
Page 10 – From *Life* Mag 13th Jan 1961. Source: books.google.com/books?id=zUUEAAAAMBAJ&printsec (PD image).*
Page 11 – From *Life* Mag 17th Mar 1961. Source: books.google.com/books?id=vUUEAAAAMBAJ&printsec (PD image).*
Page 12 – Image cropped from Edison Electric Institute advertisement in *Life* Magazine, 7th Apr 1961. Source: books.google.com/ books?id=-FEEAAAAMBAJ&printsec (PD image).*
Page 13 – Civil rights marches on Washington DC. 28th Aug 1963. From the US Library of Congress Prints & Photographs division. Sources: loc.gov/item/2003654395/ by Leffler, Warren K. and loc.gov/resource/ppmsca.37245/ by Trikosko, Marion S. (PD images).
Page 14 – Still image from the video *Life In 60's Britain* by Chaz Mork.** Source: youtube.com/watch?v=pH0kvxCfvG8.
Page 15 – Source: poster-shop.com/anonym/kunst-auf-mass-piccadilly-circus-london-1960-von-anonym.html Creator unknown. Pre 1978, no copyright mark (PD image).
Page 16 – From *Life* Mag 13th Jan 1961. Source: books.google.com/books?id=zUUEAAAAMBAJ&printsec (PD image).*
Page 17 – Lady on a London Bus, 1960. Photographer unknown. Pre 1978, no copyright mark (PD image).
– The Beatles on the Ed Sullivan Show, 9th Feb 1964, by CBS. Source: commons.wikimedia.org/wiki/File:Beatles_with_Ed_Sullivan. jpg. Pre 1978, no copyright mark (PD image).
Page 18 – From *Life* Mag 6th Jan 1961. Source: books.google.com/books?id=yEUEAAAAMBAJ&printsec (PD image).*
Page 19 – Image from *Life* Magazine Pontiac advert, 6th Oct 1961. Source: books.google.com/books?id=01MEAAAAMBAJ&printsec. (PD image).* – Steaknshake, source: web.archive.org/web/20080801225201/http://www.steaknshake.com/history.asp. Pre 1978, no copyright mark (PD image).
Page 20 – 1961 Chrysler and Chevy Corvair advertisements (cropped) from *Life* Magazine 3rd March 1961. Source: books.google.com/books?id=wUUEAAAAMBAJ&printsec (PD image).*
Page 21 – Renault from *Life* Mag 3rd Mar 1961. Source: books.google.com/books?id=wUUEAAAAMBAJ&printsec (PD image).* – Morris Minor (1961) by Andrew Bone. Source: flickr.com/photos/andreboeni/40815768332/. 4.0 Int (CC BY 4.0). – Volkswagen (1961) from *Life* Mag 5th May. Source: books.google.com/books?id=qE8EAAAAMBAJ&printsec (PD image).*
Page 22 – From *Life* Mag 6th Jan 1961. Source: books.google.com/books?id=yEUEAAAAMBAJ&printsec (PD image).*
Page 23 – From *Life* Mag 7th July 1961. Source: books.google.com/books?id=WFQEAAAAMBAJ&printsec (PD image).*
Page 24 – From *Life* Mag Motorola Ad 6th Oct 1961. Source: books.google.com/books?id=01MEAAAAMBAJ&printsec (PD image).*
Page 25 – *Wagon Train* publicity photo by Revue Studios, Dec 1962. Source: en.wikipedia.org/wiki/File:Robert_Horton_ Ward_Bond_Wagon_Train.JPG. Pre 1978, no copyright mark (PD image).
– Still image from *Gunsmoke* by CBS.** – Clint Eastwood in *Rawhide*.** Source: commons.wikimedia.org/wiki/File:Clint_Eastwood_Don_Hight_ Rawhide_1962.JPG.
Page 26 – *Dr. Kildaire* publicity photo, 1961, by NBC Tel. Source: en.wikipedia.org/wiki/Dr._Kildare_(TV_series) (PD image). – *Mr. Ed* publicity photo, circa 1962, by CBS. Source: en.wikipedia.org/wiki/File:Mister_Ed_main_cast_2.JPG (PD image). – *Ben Casey*, 1961, by ABC Films. Source: archivtv.cz/-vince-edwards. Pre 1978, no copyright mark (PD image). – *Password*, photo of Allen Ludden from *The Best of Password, The CBS Years: 1961-1967*, 3 Disc Set 30-episode DVDs.**
Page 27 – Source: flickr.com/photos/91591049@N00/15796010030/. Pre 1978, no mark (PD image).*
Page 28 – *The Dick Van Dyke Show* publicity photos by CBS Television. Petrie family 1963, and Van Dyke and Moore 1961, source: en.wikipedia.org/wiki/The_Dick_Van_Dyke_Show (PD images).
Page 29 – *The New Dick Van Dyke Show* publicity photo by CBS Television. Source: en.wikipedia.org/wiki/The_New_Dick_ Van_Dyke_Show. Pre 1978, no copyright mark (PD image).
– *The Mary Tyler Moore Show* publicity photo by CBS Television in 1970. Source: en.wikipedia.org/wiki/File:Mary_Tyler_Moore_cast_1970.jpg. Pre 1978, no copyright mark (PD image).
Page 30 – U. S. Army Signal Corps photo in the John F. Kennedy Presidential Library and Museum, Boston. Acc Number: PX65-108-CC18209. Source: jfklibrary.org/media/9471. This image is a work of a US Government employee (PD image).
Page 31 – The Kennedys with Sinatra, by Abbie Rowe, National Park Service. Photo from the John F. Kennedy Presidential Library and Museum, Boston. Source: en.wikipedia.org/wiki/File:John_F._Kennedy_Inaugural_Ball,_20_January_1961.jpg. This image is a work of a United States Government employee (PD image). – Official White House photo, 20th Feb 1961. Source: commons.wikimedia.org/wiki/John_F._Kennedy. This image is a work of a US Government employee (PD image).
Page 32 – From *Life* Mag 6th Oct 1961. Source: books.google.com/books?id=01MEAAAAMBAJ&printsec (PD image).*
Page 34 – Chernushka, circa 1961. Source: dirkdeklein.net/2018/03/09/ivan-ivanovich-unsung-space-hero/. – Gagarin, source: tass.com/society/899827 by Valentin Cheredintsev. – Tereshkova, source: cultura.biografieonline.it/la-prima-donna-nello-spazio/. – Leonov source: cultura.biografieonline.it/riferimenti/unione-sovietica/. All images this page Pre- 1978, no copyright mark (PD images).

Page 35 – Shepard, 5th May 1961, by NASA. Source: nasa.gov/topics/history/milestones/spacesuit.html. (PD image).
– Aldrin, by NASA. Source: nasa.gov/mission_pages/apollo/40th/images/apollo_image_12.html. (PD image).
Page 36 – *Battle of the Worlds* poster art 1961, by Cinema International.** Source: moriareviews.com/sciencefiction/battle-of-the-worlds-1961.htm. – *The Phantom Planet* poster art 1961, by American International.**
Source: en.wikipedia.org/wiki/The_Phantom_Planet. – *Nude on the Moon* poster art 1961, by J.E.R.**
Source: en.wikipedia.org/ wiki/Nude_on_the_Moon. – *Invasion of the Neptune Men* poster art 1961, by Toei Company (Japan).** Source: en.wikipedia.org/wiki/Invasion_of_the_Neptune_Men.
Page 37 – Castro, cropped image from Che Guevara & Fidel Castro by Alberto Korda - Museo Che Guevara, Havana Cuba, 1961. Source: en.wikipedia.org/wiki/Fidel_Castro (PD image). – Prisoners, 17th April 1961. Source: latinamericanstudies. org/bay-of-pigs/2506-prisoners.jpg. Pre 1978, no copyright mark (PD image). – Kennedys, 29th Dec 1962. Source: commons. wikimedia. org/wiki/ File:Kennedy_greet_2506_Brigade_(1962-12-29).jpg. Pre 1978, no copyright mark (PD image).
Page 38 – Construction of the Berlin Wall, from the National Archives. Source: commons.wikimedia.org/wiki/File: Berlin_ Wall_1961-11-20.jpg (PD image). – Brandenburg Gate by SSGT F. Lee Corkran, from DoD photo, USA. Source: commons. wikimedia. org/wiki/ File:BrandenburgerTorDezember1989.jpg. This image is a work of a US Government employee (PD).
Page 39 – Green Beret in Vietnam, 1961, from *Life* Magazine. Source: sofrep.com/news/jfk-sends-400-green-beret-special-advisors-may-1961-begin-vietnam-involvement/. Pre 1978, no copyright mark (PD image).
– US choppers, 1962, from *Life* Magazine. Source: 1960sdaysofrage.wordpress.com/2017/10/24/operation-chopper/. Pre 1978 (PD image).
Page 40 – From *Life* Mag 3rd Mar. Source: books.google.com/books?id=wUUEAAAAMBAJ&printsec. (PD image).*
Page 41 – Burning bus, courtesy Birmingham Civil Rights Institute. Pre 1978, no copyright mark (PD image).
– Freedom Riders police mug-shots, courtesy Mississippi Department of Archives and History. Pre 1978, no copyright mark (PD image).
Page 42 – From *Life* Mag 3rd Nov 1961. Source: books.google.com/books?id=flMEAAAAMBAJ&printsec. (PD image).*
Page 44 – Cool-Ray Polaroid Sunglasses print advertisement. Source: Ebay. (PD image).*
Page 45 – From *Life* Mag 3rd Nov 1961. Source: books.google.com/books?id=flMEAAAAMBAJ&printsec. (PD image).*
Page 46 – Screen still from the movie *El Cid*, Allied Artists 1961.**
Page 47 – *The Guns of Navarone* movie poster, Columbia Pictures 1961.**
Source: commons.m.wikipedia.org/wiki/The_Guns_of_Navarone_(film). – *One Hundred & One Dalmatians* movie poster, Disney 1961.** Source: en.wikipedia.org/wiki/One_ Hundred_and_One_Dalmatians.
– *El Cid* movie poster, Allied Artists 1961.** – Warren Beatty, 1961 photographer unknown.
Source: commons.m.wikipedia.org/wiki/File:Warren_Beatty_Photoplay,_1961.jpg. Pre 1978 (PD image).
Page 48 – *West Side Story* Italian release film poster 1961.** – Natalie Wood 26th Oct 1959, by Elmer Holloway for NBC Television. Source: commons.wikimedia.org/wiki/File:Natalie_Wood_1959_photo.jpg. Pre 1978, no copyright mark (PD image). – Beymer, circa 1960, creator unknown. Pre 1978, no copyright mark (PD image).
Page 49 – *Confidential*, Jan 1961 magazine cover. – *Inside Story* May 1961 magazine cover. – *Uncensored*, Oct 1961 magazine cover. – *Movie Life Yearbook* 1961 magazine cover. All images this page pre-1978, no copyright (PD images).
Page 50 – From *Life* Mag 13th Jan 1961. Source: books.google.com/books?id=zUUEAAAAMBAJ&printsec (PD image).*
Page 51 – From *Life* Mag 1st Sep 1961. Source: books.google.com/books?id=rVQEAAAAMBAJ&printsec (PD image).*
Page 52 – Movie poster for Ocean's 11, by Warner Bros, 1960.**
– Sinatra publicity photo by CBS. 1966, and Martin, Garland, Sinatra from The Judy Garland Show in 1962.**
Source: commons.wikimedia.org/wiki/Category:Frank_Sinatra.
Page 53 – The Supremes, 30th Sept 1965 by Jac. de Nijs / Anefo - Nationaal Archief, CC0.
Source: commons.wikimedia.org/w/index.php?curid=33712884. Pre 1978 (PD image). – The Beatles in Milan, 1965.
Source: it.wikipedia.org/wiki/File:Beatles_duomo. Photographer unknown. Pre 1978, no copyright mark (PD image).
Page 54 – Patsy Cline publicity photo, March 1957. Source: en.wikipedia.org/wiki/Patsy_Cline. Pre 1978 (PD image).
– Chubby Checker, unknown author, photo 1964.
Source: commons.wikimedia.org/wiki/File:Chubby_Checker_1964.jpg. Pre 1978 (PD image).
– Roy Orbison photo from the Nederlands Nationaal Archief, 25th March 1965.
Source: commons.wikimedia.org/wiki/File:Roy_Orbison_(1965).jpg by Jac. de Nijs / Anefo. Attribution 4.0 International License. – Del Shannon publicity photo for Amy Records in *Billboard*, 7th Aug 1965. Source: en.wikipedia.org/wiki/Del_ Shannon#/media/File:Del_Shannon_1965.jpg. Pre 1978 (PD image).
Page 55 – Connie Francis publicity photo, 17th Aug 1961. Source: commons.wikimedia.org/wiki/File:Connie_Francis_1961.JPG by ABC Television. Pre 1978 (PD image).
– The Shirelles, Billboard ad by *Scepter Records*, 24th Nov 1962. Source:
commons.wikimedia.org/wiki/Category:The_Shirelles#/media/File:The_Shirelles_1962.jpg. Pre 1978, (PD image).
Page 56 – Lana Lobell Home Catalog Spring 1961. Pre 1978, no copyright mark (PD image).
Page 57 –2-piece suit from the Wool Bureau advertisement, from *Life* Magazine, 8th Feb 1960. Source: books.google.com/books? id=-EoEAAAAMBAJ&printsec (PD image).* – Models in tea dresses, 1960s. (PD image).

Page 58 – Jacqueline Kennedy photo by Cecil Stoughton, White House, 17th Mar 1962. From the John F. Kennedy Presidential Library and Museum, Boston. Source: commons.wikimedia.org/wiki/File:Mrs._Kennedy%27s_trip_to_India._Udaipur,_Rajasthan,_cruise_on_Lake_Pichola.jpg. Property of the United States Government in the public domain. – Kennedy at the Elysee Palace, France, 31st May 1961, from the JFK Library. Source: commons.wikimedia.org/wiki/File:President_De_Gaulle_stands_between_President_Kennedy_and_Mrs._Kennedy_on_the_steps_of_the_Elysee_Palace.jpg (PD image). – Jaqueline Kennedy at the US Embassy, New Delhi, March 12-21, 1962. Source: flickr.com/photos/54323860@N06/6914524677. Attribution-NoDerivatives 4.0 International (CC BY-ND 4.0). – Italian fashions from 1960, creator unknown. Source: moda.com/fashion-history/60s-italian-fashion-1.shtml, reproduced under terms of Fair Use. Images here are significant to the article and are rendered in low resolution to avoid piracy. It is believed that these images will not in any way limit the ability of the copyright owners to sell their product.

Page 59 – Avon 1961 by Nesster. Source: flickr.com/photos/nesster/35520707662/ (PD image).*

Page 60 – From *Life* Mag 6th Oct 1961. Source: books.google.com/books?id=01MEAAAAMBAJ&printsec (PD image).*

Page 61 – Photo Mods of the early 1960s. Source unknown. Pre 1978 (PD image). – Models in Mary Quant mini dresses, creator unknown. Source: thedabbler.co.uk/2012/10/granny-takes-a-trip-back-in-time/. Pre 1978 (PD image). – Mary Quant, 16 Dec 1966. Source: commons.wikimedia.org/wiki/File:Mary_Quant_in_a_minidress_(1966).jpg by Jac. de Nijs / Anefo. Image from the Nationaal Archief, the Dutch National Archives, licensed under the Creative Commons Attribution-Share Alike 3.0 Netherlands.

Page 62 – Penelope Tree, photographer Richard Avedon for Vogue Oct 1967. – Jean Shrimpton for Australian Vogue August 1965, Twiggy for Italian Vogue, July 1967, and various photo of Twiggy, dates, photographers, source unknown. Images reproduced this page under terms of Fair Use are used sparingly for information only, are significant to the article created and are rendered in low resolution to avoid piracy. It is believed that these images will not in any way limit the ability of the copyright owners to sell their product.

Page 63 – Models wearing fashions from the late '60s. Photographers unknown. Pre 1978, (PD images). – The Beatles. Source: commons.wikimedia.org/wiki/File:The_Beatles_magical_mystery_tour.jpg. Attribution 3.0 (CC BY 3.0).

Page 64 – From *Life* Mag 13th Jan 1961. Source: books.google.com/books?id=zUUEAAAAMBAJ&printsec (PD image).*

Page 65 – From *Life* Mag 24th Feb 1961. Source: books.google.com/books?id=zkgEAAAAMBAJ&printsec (PD image).*

Page 66 – Player, cropped press photo in 1961, creator unknown. Source: commons.wikimedia.org/wiki/File:Gary_Player_with_wife_and_her_mother_1961.jpg. Pre 1978, no copyright mark (PD image). – Laver at 1969 Top Tennis Tournament in Amsterdam, by Evers, Joost / Anefo - Nationaal Archief Fotocollectie Anefo item number 922-4468. Source: en.wikipedia.org/wiki/Rod_Laver#/media/File:Rodney_George_Laver.jpg. Pre 1978, no copyright mark (PD image). – Moss in his winning Lotus-Climax at the 1961 German Grand Prix, by Lothar Spurzem, 6th Aug 1961. Source: commons.wikimedia.org/wiki/File:MossLotusClimax19610806.jpg. Licensed under the Creative Commons Attribution-Share Alike 2.0 Germany.

Page 67 – Selectric II dual Latin/Hebrew Hadar element by Etan J. Tal, source: en.wikipedia.org/wiki/IBM_Selectric_typewriter#/media/File:SelectricII_Hadar.jpg. 3.0 Unported (CC BY 3.0). – Unimate, from the Automated Manufacturing Research Facility, National Institute of Standards & Technology. Source: commons.wikimedia.org/ wiki/Category:National_ Institute_of_Standards_and_Technology#/media/File:AutomatedManufacturingResearchFacility_011.jpg (PD image).

Page 68 – Farthing, 1951. Source: en.wikipedia.org/wiki/Farthing_(British_coin). Pre 1978, no copyright mark (PD image). – Operation Vantage. Source: commandoveterans.org/42_Commando_RM_archive?items_per_page=All. (PD image). – Hemmingway, 1939, source: commons.wikimedia.org/wiki/Ernest_Hemingway#/media/File:ErnestHemingway.jpg (PD).

Page 69 – 800 women strikers for peace on 47 St near the UN Bldg. From Library of Congress Digital ID: cph 3c28465 hdl.loc.gov/loc.pnp/cph.3c28465 (PD image). – Portuguese Soldiers Surrendering to Indian Army, from Government Museum, Panaji. Source: kamat.com/database/content/goa_freedom/16342.htm. Pre 1978 no copyright mark (PD image).

Page 70 – From *Life* Mag 26th May 1961. Source: books.google.com/books?id=rk8EAAAAMBAJ&printsec (PD image).*

Page 71 – From *Life* Mag 7th July 1961. Source: books.google.com/books?id=WFQEAAAAMBAJ&printsec (PD image).*

Page 72-74 – All photos are, where possible, CC BY 2.0 or PD images made available by the creator for free use including commercial use. Where commercial use photos are unavailable, photos are included here for information only under U.S. fair use laws due to: 1- images are low resolution copies; 2- images do not devalue the ability of the copyright holders to profit from the original works in any way; 3- Images are too small to be used to make illegal copies for use in another book; 4- The images are relevant to the article created.

Page 75 – From *Life* Mag 6th Jan 1961. Source: books.google.com/books?id=yEUEAAAAMBAJ&printsec (PD image).*

Page 78 – From *Life* Mag 6th Oct 1961. Source: books.google.com/books?id=01MEAAAAMBAJ&printsec (PD image).*

Page 79 – From *Life* Mag 26th May 1961. Source: books.google.com/books?id=rk8EAAAAMBAJ&printsec (PD image).*

*Advertisement (or image from an advertisement) is in the public domain because it was published in a collective work (such as a periodical issue) in the US between 1925 and 1977 and without a copyright notice specific to the advertisement.

**Posters for movies or events are either in the public domain (published in the US between 1925 and 1977 and without a copyright notice specific to the artwork) or owned by the production company, creator, or distributor of the movie or event. Posters, where not in the public domain, and screen stills from movies or TV shows, are reproduced here under USA Fair Use laws due to: 1- images are low resolution copies; 2- images do not devalue the ability of the copyright holders to profit from the original works in any way; 3- Images are too small to be used to make illegal copies for use in another book; 4- The images are relevant to the article created.

This book was written by Bernard Bradforsand-Tyler as part of
A Time Traveler's Guide series of books.

All rights reserved. The author exerts the moral right to be identified as the author of the work.

No parts of this book may be reproduced, stored in any retrieval system, or transmitted in any form or by any means, without prior written permission from the author.

This is a work of nonfiction. No names have been changed, no events have been fabricated. The content of this book is provided as a source of information for the reader, however it is not meant as a substitute for direct expert opinion. Although the author has made every effort to ensure that the information in this book is correct at time of printing, and while this publication is designed to provide accurate information in regard to the subject matters covered, the author assumes no responsibility for errors, inaccuracies, omissions, or any other inconsistencies herein and hereby disclaims any liability to any party for any loss, damage, or disruption caused by errors or omissions.

All images contained herein are reproduced with the following permissions:
- Images included in the public domain.
- Images obtained under creative commons license.
- Images included under fair use terms.
- Images reproduced with owner's permission.

All image attributions and source credits are provided at the back of the book. All images are the property of their respective owners and are protected under international copyright laws.

First printed in 2020 in the USA (ISBN 979-8561076411).
Revised in 2021, 2nd Edition (ISBN 978-0-6450623-5-9).
Revised in 2024, 3rd Edition (ISBN 978-1-922676-30-6).
Self-published by B. Bradforsand-Tyler.

www.ingramcontent.com/pod-product-compliance
Lightning Source LLC
Chambersburg PA
CBHW070321120526
44590CB00017B/2763